THE PENDULUM
MOVES OFF

poems

THE PENDULUM MOVES OFF

poems

Theodore Haddin

MADVILLE
PUBLISHING

Lake Dallas, Texas

Permissions
Madville Publishing
PO Box 358
Lake Dallas, TX 75065

Cover Design: Kimberly Davis
Cover Art: *The Sower* by Vincent Van Gogh, 1889

ISBN: 978-1-956440-67-6 paperback
978-1-956440-68-3 ebook
Library of Congress Control Number: 2023944063

To Peter and Mandy,
Leslie and Burt, Sarah and Christopher

TABLE OF CONTENTS

I

II

III

IV

V

I

FIRST MOVES

At three he is out in the yard
squatting in the grass, looking
at something. From the kitchen
his mother sees him squatting.
She comes out and quietly
approaches to look; he is
watching ants come out of
an anthill, from a single hole
at the center, go out and around,
and go back with something.
She quietly returns to her kitchen.

Grandfather winds the clock
as if winding all times ahead,
though it is only for a week.
The pendulum stands and waits
for time to go. The boy thinks
each swing will take it ahead,
while the pendulum with
the other swing takes it back,
the reason for winding Saturday
nights. The pendulum moves
its inevitable swing so slowly
he begins to comprehend how
tock and tick will accompany
him forever. It's always a time
coming; he doesn't yet think of
how it will be passing.

Raspberries and Milk

It's always sudden green, a whole field
of grass, so green right up to a gray building
with no windows. It could be a barn or a house.
The grass is always long, and nothing is
at home. The grandparents are somewhere,
but you can't see them. It's summer,
a warm afternoon that makes the green intense
and fragrant. I've tried to think of what this
means, always coming to me as if some meaning
waits in this incredible green. The grandfather's
new Hudson Terraplane (1936), a great metalwork
with huge bulbous fenders speaks of earth and
sky that don't match the car's outrageous
purple. He's somewhere shining it as if Sundays
go on forever. Near a fence next door I am
picking raspberries red and black. Their owner,
an older Black woman, sweetly calls me to ask
if I would like some berries with sugar and milk.
The grandmother doesn't want me to go into her
house. I enter anyway. Her kitchen smells warm
like sweat. She is so kind, she pours the milk and
loads the sugar. I feel the grass now, rich and free,
in my bare feet. The grandmother knows where I am;
somehow I can't hear her calling me to come back in.

Winter Came

Winter came, and there was no heat
on that porch. The pots of geraniums
in the sills had to survive by what
winter sunlight came through tall
windows that opened to half the room.
And there sat my Boy Scout first aid
kit from August to April—when first
thaws began to melt snows along
the roof and driveway—a forgotten
can along with summer's playthings,
now full of worms, full because they
had multiplied, through the long and dark
winter days and nights and had come
a thrashing and squirming red ball
of incredible life. They would be
bluegill bait in another time, but
when the first patch of green showed
amid the melting snow, I would take
the can out, open it, and release that
squirming ball to their new life in our
back lawn. Maybe I would see some
of them later as I trimmed grass on
my hands and knees. The robins
would come for sure. Something
about letting them go, let go of
something in me then, and I was happy
about worms and earth and melting snows.

Awakening

A story is sometimes told
of wise men who took something
from outside or from the past
that changed their lives.
One spring morning in May,
walking up the long street
to my school, I felt something
around me. It was so strong
I turned around to look.
The buds of green leaves
on all the young maple trees
that lined the street,
forming a perfect green mist,
had enclosed me while I walked.
Now I took it in. It was so beautiful
I didn't wish harm to any thing.
I stood for several minutes.
I stepped into a side street
to see if my feeling was still there.
Then I reentered the mist.
Not all the metal and concrete
I could see could interfere
with what it means to live on Earth,
where I was, what I was to be.

Rembrandt's Wheel Ruts

It was either in early spring
or in late fall; the traditional fenceposts
are there in a row, looking old,
and the fields weather-worn,
the lines at the horizon slanting up
to make trees and shrubs of a shrubby life
come up stark, slanting sunset rays
you can't see, but feel, in the background,
and then these sepia lines that roll over
in a tumble, the great curving ruts of the mud,
that we can't mistake for mere ant-scratch,
with three long brown lines that cut straight
across all the others that run away,
they are the weather itself,
and this, this is the road.

What's It Like to Have a Violin

What's it like to have a violin.
Take advantage of the sun.
I'm wild about my violin.
So what if not a Stradivarius,
no difference to the sun.
Shine, and clean, polish,
tune, bow-upon-string,
Bach, Bach, and Beethoven,
Mozart, Handel, and Vivaldi,
as the great ones reach us,
fingers free to make their runs
as we sing with strings in our
lonely rooms. One day someone
hears music from all we've done.
What's it like to have a violin.
Take advantage of the sun.

MOCKINGBIRD WHY DO YOU

Mockingbird, he's a ground bird, really,
who likes the vantage point of a tree.
Silent, he sits atop a twig. Then down
he goes at a speck in the grass I can't see.
Something he gets, once or twice, and never
a sound makes he, while I sing him
twelve songs to his eye, not his ear.
But come midnight I see how I was wrong.
He appears at my window to know if I'm in.
The way he does this is to sing those twelve songs,
one after the other as if recorded to perform.
I listen and wonder about him, his silly notion
of coming back so late to show he can sing.
He may be the true musical lover on wing.
Yet it's the part about memory I ponder most,
whether he's showing off or sharing in his peculiar way,
or desperate to say he can't sing an original song.

WINTER WASH

I

I was trying to tell old Norman
what it was like, and he kept
saying he didn't believe in snow,
till I told him this: In winter
we used to hang the wash outside.
It was cold, and crusts of ice
on the line encircled my mother's
panties. White shirts of three men
were indistinguishable from snow,
sheets the same. Pants hung dead
stiff. And then there was the cold
basement where the ancient washer
whirled and knocked till we squeezed
the clothes through a wringer turned
with a crank and dropped them
into rinsing tubs of murky lukewarm
and cold waters. Outside awaited
lines frozen with ice. I would carry up
the heavy baskets of wet clothes for
my mother who could not manage them.
Three days to a week out there. If we
had to hang in the cellar, the lines
might receive benefits of the off-and-on
furnace that afforded some warmth. But
I remember dodging laundry hanging
there all winter—clothes never seemed
to end their drying. All because of snow.

II

Came April one year snow and ice
began to melt and air took on
a freshness of spring coming. One day
out there, we heard a loud cracking,
as if Walden Pond were opening up,
and from down below a shrill voice
called out, "I made it!" A screen door
ripped open. A long spud chopped
at ice. Out of frozen melee struggled
a little old lady, our neighbor Mrs.
McConnell, whom we hadn't seen
since the first snow, still in her house
robe, and strands of scraggly gray hair
taggling in the wind. Suddenly fully
emerged, she cried out again, "I made
it! I made it!" And throwing down
the heavy spud, she raised her arms wide
and cried again, "I made it!" From
a snowy embankment we called down to
her for the first time and let her know
we'd be down soon with something you
won't mistake for ice or snow—some
hot soup and a chocolate cake.

GRANDPA WEARS NECKTIES

He stood his usual grinning self
before the mirror with his new bowtie.
"I can do this easy," he says, and begins
to wrap two ends tight about his collar.
Then whatever slipped stuck in knot.
He looked at it and went right on
as if to finish the job. But it twisted,
it didn't turn, it caught his finger.
He was struggling with a snake.
He gritted his teeth.
At last he had to admit he couldn't
do it. He hated what to do next.
He sought the scissors in the kitchen
and held one end of the rascal till he
could cut it all off, blue Blenheim
it was, Churchill's favorite, shredded
to the floor, as if old buildings had
fallen in London. But he was so far
from the London streets now he'd
never go back. Then off for a necktie,
black, and carefully wrapped it,
pulled it back. He couldn't be seen
doing this. With his foot he kicked
at the scraps.

SUNDAY AFTERNOON

I was always throwing a baseball
directly above the handle's door,
only it wasn't a baseball then
but a tennis ball hit the mark
that kept my father from knowing
what his son was doing by himself,
and a neighbor came to throw me one.
The baseball stayed in my glove
alone, as I was alone, with my dream
of George Kell's magnificent throws
across the diamond to even the score,
catches he made straight above ground,
while the crowd went wild about him,
and he was proudly hitting three twenty-four.

LINES FOR MAURICE McNAMEE, SJ

(The Dream That Catches On)

There I was, at the Jesuit Residence,
out on the diamond, playing center field.
I could see the pitches as they rose or curved
toward the plate. It was the freshest of green
as all around 'twas just beginning of spring.
Father Joe Knapp had gone out already.
Then Father Mac came up, his usual smiling self,
and I just heard him to the catcher,
"It's going up there," and he planted his cleats
firm in the batter's box. When that final pitch came,
he made a mighty swing, his shoulders rising,
his game leg straightened with the bat,
and I saw a ball coming up over the diamond
rising in my direction and I prepared to receive it,
but I had no glove and the ball was turning
marvelously fast and went up over my head
out of sight. We weren't playing the usual way.
For some brief seconds the sky had McNamee
written all over it. The game was over,
and somebody had won.

Messiaen's Quartet for the End of Time

for Craig Hultgren

I look through the window this day
and see the garden, oh garden of gardens
like our Earth that may be the last one
on the last day the cypress vine has
overtaken the tomatoes and Japanese eggplants
oh taken over all with its rosemary-like
green leaves and tiny red flowers white
at their centers hundreds and hundreds now
so deeply green and red and bright in the sun's
light I will go out there I say
I will go out among blades and blooms
and stand between tall tomato sticks and vines
and when I am there come sulfur butterflies
one by one and five by five and thirty all alight
and perch on my head and shoulders as if I were
a plant to please by giving and taking from the white
dot at the center of red flowers and the players
and I are taken in, one by one, our depths sounded
in long meditations as our new music renders them
and butterflies know what we are playing.

BROTHERS

I Hunting

We started out picking our guns for rabbits,
nothing too big, nothing too small. We didn't
want a load of pellets at the cleaning. He
took the four-ten, and I took his semi-automatic
twenty-two. It was an overcast fall day.
We had to go through fields where rabbits ran.
Maybe I would see a pheasant. When we came
to the fence that bordered the woods, we put
our guns down to make the crossing, Paul first,
then his gun. I went over easily, then reached
for mine. Now on the other side, I lifted
the twenty-two, and for a split-second it came in
range of his back. I don't know how to tell
what happened next. The gun suddenly went off
with a loud bang. I hadn't touched the trigger.
The bullet whizzed between his right ear and
the hair of his head, just lifting the edge of his
hunting cap. He turned then, startled beyond
belief, a look of horror that I might have so
misfired. The safety had been on. Puzzled
what I couldn't explain about its erratic muzzle,
I handed him the gun.

II At the Thornapple

We went down a long way to the river
one day, through woods, over tarmac
that burned and blackened the bottoms
of our feet, and over an old field of alfalfa
where we heard at our backs the hoof
and snort of an angry black bull just as
we ascended a barbed-wire fence.
We couldn't have felt more welcomed

by being at the river's edge. Will, the
friend, went right out, his arms flailing.
Brother Paul, with his he-man's bluster,
turned back to chop wood for fire.
I unpacked. It was late afternoon.
A sickle of moon rose behind us at odds
with the receding sun. I had taken off
my shirt to dig a firepit. It was not
an owl's call from the woods but a whoop-
whoop coming close to my ear, presently
a wind, and the unwinding loops of
an axe going by swish-swish all the way
to the river and in. It had just missed.
I, too, turned then. Something he had
saved up when I least expected it?
Were we supposed to say what bothered
us about being brothers, or keep it to
ourselves for these unknown moments?
Something underlay our rough chances.
He wanted to know how close he could
come to me. I had my doubts about
how close I could come to him.

III Coda

Long after that day the gun went off,
and that axe had sunk in mud
where we would never know,
I am looking out the window
of a garage in winter. From nowhere
comes into the yard a magnificent
ring-necked pheasant. He's after
the berries in the junipers. The blue-black
sheen of his neck and the brilliant red
at his throat are bright against
the whiteness of snow. When I
look at his tracks, I want to open
the window, but it's closed.

ARVO PÄRT PLAYS FROM THE RADIO

Arvo Pärt plays from the radio
Fratres, and the old cricket sings feebly
from the furnace, heat is on, he finds
himself still singing sleepily. I hear him
in the night bleeper bleep,
and the long strains of *Fratres* come
groaning in the cellos violas viols,
ascending ever so slow, linking
each groan each note old hymn in him,
a church where a crowd of people, their
dark coats come, they are about to sing
fratres, will you come fratres fratres.

WHERE POETRY GOES

The subject of poetry has become our motions.
It doesn't matter, the street corner crowd,
the work of ants in the garden, dry grass
caught fire, my uncle's hunting habits,
the last time I saw a cinema, watching
the stars come out at night, feeling waves
rise up to our bodies, oh anything, lost love,
the motion we made as we exited the relationship,
and just how far memory can go back into when,
and now my ear at the cell phone while I'm
driving, the circle we make between work
and after work, from box house and back again.
I'd like to include just the motion of seeing,
to whatever we turn our attention to, that makes
us think it's all a poem, and not just us saying
look, look, as if it were the last day, and we'd
better, before it's all gone and we can't see anything.

A Tale

Arpad D'Zurko had a Guarnerius.
He left it in a tavern, so he said.
The wild music lay in a box
somewhere, and he prayed
his prayers in Gypsy
till newspapers caught his words.
After a while the violin was heard
from the mouth of a bistro
in Brooklyn, a long way
from Transylvania. D'Zurko went
in, took the violin and played it
boldly only the way he could,
and it was understood it was his.
But of all the possibilities
for such an amazing instrument
the story has another ending:
The cab driver who found it thought
of a million-dollar condominium
he could have and sold it to a realtor
who had an eye for old things.
Still another version passed around,
a boy who had aspirations found a box
in an alley in Brooklyn and took it up
to his teacher who said play my boy
and at fourteen a virtuoso went out
on the streets of Brooklyn with a violin
sounding like a Gypsy.

II

PREDICTION

Word had gone abroad
they were no longer fighting.
Someone had told the president
it wasn't worth it to get
behind the long history
of Jewish-Middle Eastern conflict,
it wasn't worth the people's lives
to sacrifice all the oil
that remained to the other people.
So new names came in: Christopher
Hogwood, Messiaen, Bernstein,
Bob Dylan came back, the war
was over, Cadillacs moved over,
hybrid engines replaced even
by the newer solar cars, music
became the listener, Iranians
offered artwork, the belligerent
past floated away on a requiem
of Mozart, and green fields reappeared.
Neighbors hummed and smiled,
the way was at last found, though
greed did not disappear nor did
insider trading, but the more music
was played, the more war began to fade.

THE BOY FISHING

It's July, sky overcast,
faint sour smell of overheated
leaves drying and waiting for rain.
He thinks of casting his line out
as cars and trucks groan past him
on the road, walking where he is,
with the world moving around him.
He would like to get at the essence,
if he could, of what makes him think
he would find a fish in all this rush
and roar, a fishing pole stuck up
with a line and reel he holds
for dear life and life to come.
Something in the air
has touched his insides,
a fish is swimming still
in the deep pond of his longing.
He will be there in a while.
Worms fresh from the manure pile
hanker for hooks he'll lose
when the big one bites.
Oil and motorboats won't stop him
as his bare feet slide
past lily pads and plastic castaways
to reach their penetration in mud
where his feet at last,
and water, are one.

A Tall Tale

for John Knoepfle

I've pondered for years that Huck Finn
could tell the tale how he and Jim
caught a 200-pound catfish so big
it could throw them into Illinois,
"as big a fish as was ever catched
in the Mississippi." Their task,
they thought, was to let it
thrash around until it drowned.
A fish that big could have run away
with their raft. It all depends on
what you want to believe. Usually,
Huck just says, "We caught some fish
and had a hot breakfast," but this
whopper hit their line, that must have
been made of steel. Fishermen usually
report the line they used. There was no
struggle, the Twain of details was missing
there. They don't say how they got it
aboard, but they could measure it,
as long as a man. And here is the believer:
In its stomach Huck said they found
a brass button and a ball that held a spool.
Back then a body could say anything,
I suppose. I've wondered how big was
their raft.

Now, about a hundred years after
their time, the tale gets longer.
Walking by the Mississippi near the Arch
at St. Louis, where I could easily throw
a stone across, suddenly appeared three
scuba divers like ninjas, who banked
their canoe and calmly dived in. I

supposed it was the modern way to
fathom the Mississippi, but just as
suddenly up they came, one, two, three,
like fleeting dolphins, going for shore.
The tallest one flew toward me, his eyes
wide open, his mouth agog. "What's
going on?" I said. Barely able to speak,
he uttered, "There are catfish down there
bigger and longer than we are!" I didn't know
what to say. Had Twain struck again? To
check this tale for a few inches more, I'd
have to go down there myself. But regarding
what he had just said, I wasn't disposed
to go down there that day—or any day.

TRUTH-TELLING

To believe everything you say
doesn't necessarily make it true.
Candor is only the way to the next
encounter with your self, leaving out
the little bits we always ignore
because they make us stop
to know our own fallibility.
I believe I am honest
doesn't always make it true.
The little leftover in the corner
of my own sardine can
can never somehow be explained.
Better to say we acknowledge truth
when it hits us and go on from there.
The moment of candor is not
when we leave off dark wine or women.
Or when women leave us off. It's knowing
where you are going with either one.

Broken Heart

When your heart is broken,
you can take its parts apart
and look inside as never before,
you can try to see what made it
want more than it could do.
So you think of how to put it
back together. No Humpty
Dumpty here, you have to go on
what was broken in the first place,
and maybe it was only cracks
you have to get used to, to avoid
future attacks. Or, you might try
a valvotomy, a coronary bypass,
a window from the ribs, or just
a stent. The other person watched
you, and you watched her, as
you slid into dissolution. Maybe
there was barking, something
like that as you rode off, tail
between your legs. What it was,
was probably you. Heartache is
always double-sided. The surgeon
can save your parts, but only you
can save you.

FOX BY THE ROAD

I

Coming up the road suddenly
see a small red fox lying beside
the curb another expressway death
he with his longtail I at my wheel
whatever beset him to lie there
this evening so still a sudden sight
for me driving toward a traffic light
I see his ears like a dog's sticking up
his legs straight out as if about to jump
a fence he couldn't make, a headlight
that flashed him shut O small fox
that barked a last yelp before a speeding wheel

II

Fox he was coming up the hill
in deep grass brown from winter
chasing a brown rabbit by the guardrail
he could not have seen the wheels whizzing past
nor know the sudden shock he would feel
when the rabbit cut across and blinding headlight
was all he saw and surprised a driver at high speed

III

Coming up the hill today small fox
is gone questions I had suddenly empty
where did he go did someone take him home
someone try to revive him did the rain
yesterday run the rill and wash him down
the sewer main was someone after his pelt
someone take a fancy to his tail or did this fox
small creature of twisted mouth just get up again
wry and cunning take him home when no one
was looking and just laugh like the trickster
he is guessing he could take another rabbit any day

WALDEN: A GLIMPSE

Piled up behind a concrete truck,
traffic all around,
waiting on the light
that can't be seen,
of all that hurries past
one second flashes a pond and a park
thoughts of Walden
its water a mirror
eyelash-shadows flowing
across ancient ripples
of sun and water,
the instant of this glimpse
so old beside a sterile building
yet all wildness lives in this:
Cars cough, trucks rumble,
tires hiss, as I turn for a moment
seen, glass of my car catches pond
and grass in the sky, says blue, says green.

What the Lake Said

Sunlight in the old cottage,
5:30 a.m. shadows in the corners
still dark, brother still sleeping,
I out the loft down into the kitchen
near the room where the folks slept,
silence across the dining room
where streaks of light just begin
and down into the cellar where the oars
are kept and an old canoe web-weft
from another time, and then to the boat
at the dock where the garter snake wakes
to my foot stepping into the bottom
and oarlocks rattling as they chink
into place beside a thwart.
I shove off then, the lake a dark mirror
and the wonder of ripples widening behind.
Just floating, you could see forever
how a lake looks like a sky and the smell
of woods and weeds and a leftover fire
made morning here, almost before the sun.
But the slower I went the more certain I was
of a great ripple behind the boat, a smooth
rising and dipping, dark and grotesque as
it followed to where I was going to fish.
As I had no specific destination I could
see them then, huge gars passing as they
hunted, a chilling sight as they erupted
in violent thrashes and splashes when they
reached the shore. I thought of the bass I
was looking for, and would I ever see them
again at another depth, in the wavering grass.

WE ALL KNOW HIM

Crow, his wings
glint in the sun.
They're all the colors
of things he eats,
black and silver-blue
red and green.
But of cars encroaching,
he seems unaware,
a large dark object
between wheels
steals a glimpse at us,
repeats pecking at the trash,
then in slow wing beats
like an old prop airplane
to drivers' amaze
knows exactly when
to lift himself off
from the streets.

FROG

In Vestavia Hills, in Birmingham, you might have
walked along a quarter-mile track at evening
and been so lucky to hear a *croak* from a small
pond fed by a tiny stream. If you answered back
in frog you heard another and another all the while
you walked. It was like a secret in the shadows
of the trees where song spoke a human need.
A kind of song *he* heard, I know, to no greater
end it seems than frog had found a human friend.
We kept this up from spring to spring
and all the summer long. A frog in the city
could only be if someone thinks he belongs.
But then they came, with dozers and earthhogs
to take the trees and burn their trunks
and shove the pond and turn the stream.
The light of the glint of the pond
was gone, and I found him flattened
in the dust of the dozer's track, his
one eye still looking up for the one time
I would see him and say what I could.
I lifted him on a piece of newspaper
and placed him on the back seat of my car
and slowly drove him home and held him
a few moments under the persimmon tree.
The eye closed over. I decided to turn him free
so placed him in the garden among soft leaves
and plants, there, still to be of use, silent and calm,
a king of frogs in the kingdom of ants.

Taking the Trees

She was in her kitchen
when it fell, the big pine
struck by lightning spiraling down
that mashed the roof above the dining room
and sent her chandelier crashing to the floor
so next day she got the roofers out
to hack and pillage shingles to make
a roof against all future falls and scares
then two weeks later twelve men came
to take all twelve trees that remained
the eighty- and ninety-year-old pines
whirring and burping through chips and dust
they went, and the cutters threw them back
into the woods to rot by day and get rats
by night this was bad enough he thought
to see his woods behind his house disappear
till this week the burping and ripping began
again across the street a whole hill of big trees
now eaten up by a machine that takes a whole tree
and today they begin on another set uphill
one of the oldest trees here going the same way
the old neighbors are cutting down their trees
fear has caught them all and trees that remember
with their rings don't know why humans say
you have to go, the humans themselves don't know why

On a Child's Waking at Night

He would come sometimes at 2 a.m.,
his little boy's feet sticking out
from his pajamas and just nudge me,
father asleep, and his blue eyes
would peer into mine in the night's
faint light from down the hallway.
"I'm cold," he would say, "I'm lonesome,"
till I rose with him and we found
ourselves in the kitchen's warm light.
We got out the bottle and the cooking pot,
warm milk and talk, man to man,
made the hour slide by, and we would
stride back to his bed with the warmth
we shared to tuck him in till dawn.
Once we thought he was lost
when he hid from us at a park.
Just as the evening sky grew dark,
he came out then, knowing
he could find his way.

Heart of the Violin

for Horst Kloss

When you open a violin
you can tell what its heart
      is like,
what the master will find as he
questions the distempered part.
The top comes off slow
and painstakingly,
you can see the base bar inside,
how it goes up and down
for the G and D, and just over,
for the soundpost's A and E.
Nothing comes from it now,
but edges are smoothed,
then clips are attached,
looking like the form
of a woman's body, both top
and back. Adjusting the neck
is key to all the rest. For
the heart is nothing you can
see, hidden deep in the old
wood's keep. But after this,
when work is complete,
down to the last tap to test
its tone, you will hear
the violin's voice for the first time
in the sound of the heart's beat.

HOUSES WE'VE BUILT

We live in the houses we've built,
the one for ourselves, no matter
how the years have gone by
the windows with their dust
look in upon us and the clocks
unwind over and over
while the gardens succeed each other
and the prize amaryllis goes down again
with the peonies and daffodils.
Come rain and high water
winds about us know what we've done
with the roof and the cellar
and the paint we put on one year.
We live in the house we've built
for ourselves, even strangers see
what we've become by the carpets
that have worn ourselves into their threads
and the chimney that's lost its fire.
We live in the houses we've built
by ourselves, and we would have left
a long time ago if the doors hadn't
welcomed us so many times when we came back
and the table hadn't been so congenial when it was set,
and the son and daughter who kept love alive
returned so often to open those doors again.

My Return

It wasn't that I didn't believe her,
it was just what she said,
your old house is gone,
the one where you lived.
A new school has taken its place.
Suddenly I see icicles hanging
from the roof, a dog barking
in the front yard, the twenty-year-old
maples that line the street. But
the house was shut off, she said—
I was taking it in. Morning glories
flourish on the front porch.
A door had been shut. She said
the whole block was gone, even
the McConnell's sunken house
at the corner, levelled. Mr. Scholten
next door is laying fish skeletons
in his garden. The old school
from 1890 with the dark wood
panels inside and wooden floors
that creaked and groaned, its
magnificent foundation blown to bits.
I am up on the roof with the janitor
looking for tennis balls. She said
they destroyed the old boiler
that had three hundred flues.
My father is falling off a ladder
near our roof and does a backflip
to land on his feet. But the day
is spring, I open the window, and
all that glorious fresh air comes in.

She said I could come back and see
the new school anytime, but I am
still peddling like crazy against
a strange neighborhood dog that
wants me and the loaf of bread
that keeps dropping pieces behind me.

HOMELESS

(3rd Ave South, Birmingham)

He entered a house to be
alone where no one would
find him,* but here a house
is more alone where its secret
lies in splintered boards and
missing doors. No woman or
child, (why am I drawn to it)
broken glass, a shredded
blanket, trash, tin can urinal.
Like a skeleton of carpenter's
last endeavors, a death's head
looks back through darkened
windows, cavernous floors,
visible planks and joists no
more the support of running
feet and a mother's tread
where children sleep. Yet old
letters and newspapers
proclaim a presence where
they scatter about. The years
have gone by now, in rain and
sun and snow, and the miracle
is still to be made. I will have
to solve the mystery of rot and
decay, of hands searching, nail
and board, for a house, not in
building, but in tearing down,
piece by piece, to find a home.

* Mark 7:24

GLENMARY MISSION

When the Sisters step into dry grass
and weeds of a rotting house,
they ask the destitute who owns it,
May we assist in recovery of your
life of the house. They believe
a mission may be moving everyone
who joins them, wherever they
build a house from within.
Cracked windows go, sun-bleached
boards disappear along with weeds,
doors are opened, a new air comes in.
Men and women volunteer as one
hand and one arm to saw and nail
and straighten doors. It is beautiful
to see the new house rising from
the wreck of weather and honest
neglect. Sheetrock in the wall, deck
with a door, steps for the bereft.
With these the Sisters share with us
blessed light they have always borne.

III

America

(2019)

Everybody wears masks,
some sit in silent rows
of small expensive seats.
Others from the other side
swear something needs
        to be done.
A troll steals light from the air,
words don't carry their meanings,
        lies go for truth.
Nothing is what it was.
Everything is something it isn't.
Confusion divides, while
wars lurk in the untruth.
A world slowly turns
toward a burning sun.
No one knows how hot
a world can be. Look
to Mars, we say, deserts
can be a great place to live.
We slowly learn how they
        are made.

Putting in the Flag

My sister sent a flag
it was the American, flat
and thin made in Taiwan
with a little cloth hook
on it for hanging from something
the day is Memorial and the President
is over in Normandy saying stern things
over 9,000 dead he hopes we'll remember
from far away here at home
while the bridge over the Arkansas
lies cracked and fallen and souls lost
by a barge that hit a stanchion in a storm
so what if Saddam thinks of one we don't know
this day may mark his end we think
from points of safety here still safe
my sister sent a flag I haven't put up yet
I've folded it on the dresser waiting
for a moment to hold it up and show it
maybe somewhere in my flowerbed
where things are still coming up
from long before winter as if to crowd the day
and make sure of remembering if we will

I WAS UP IN MY ROOM

I was up in my room almost asleep
when the broadcast came and bombs
were hitting the *Arizona* too late
for Americans to wake up
and then the President coming over
and making the Congress declare war
and me running downstairs to tell those
still asleep mother and father still
hung over from Saturday night
that was a war then scary as hell
and now NPR reports the Taliban
are more organized than we thought
and they intend to kill Americans
wherever they can and not to reveal
any secrets not tell the truth lie
every time asked write letters nobody
can trace back to jihad
and why not while they're at it
poison American farmlands
here says the announcer at NPR
like the Japanese who wanted to do it
in 1945 send balloons across the Pacific
filled with poisoned turkey feathers
microorganisms parasites to let drift
down and scatter across fields
float even as now when American farmers
say in Iowa and Kansas for a start
look up now fearing turkey feathers

How the Mississippi comes down at Vicksburg
is a long memory that hides the meaning of time
as it stumbles and repeats till it clarifies. To tell
the truth, at its source some have seen clear water
and later far down along its meandering shores.
The "Big Muddy" enters just above St. Louis
to darken waters flowing down where the Ohio
empties in. Going up and down it, Twain must
have seen *something*, cows, a chicken coop,
an abandoned house, a burning steamboat, even
a whole tree and roots floating by. Now, a rusting
Ford moves in slow sludge along with an old
box spring, gallons of waste paint, and rotting
cabbages. It doesn't have to come all at once,
it just comes. What is thrown away in the dark
no one will ever know. How long was this
a bargain of the American conscience? In the War
the poet in Lincoln wrote, "Vicksburg is the key.
The war cannot be brought to a close until the
key is in our pocket." Only, nineteen thousand
men were lost to keep it. This too, is Mississippi
and America. From here waters flow down into
marshes and a Gulf oil spill of dead and dying
oysters and coral reefs, lost turtles and birds.
The city has enough to live with. People who
don't know the content of a river can't be
separated from its flow may not change their
minds in other matters. Huge catfish still pick
over old bones of drowned slaves and tattered
uniforms. Farther down, chemical dispersants
barely tick at dark masses in deep waters.

AT THE JEFFERSON COUNTY COURTHOUSE, 1999

You could walk right past it and never see it
the men's room I mean until you see the Exit sign
and the little label under it that we're supposed
to see from way down the hallway in the Collector's room
Well he went in about the same time I did
first through the exit door then the old one
with a little sign *men* and inside it was jovial
enough with him and me standing in two latrines
you would not have thought about it until later
in the time it took for us to pee we said
good morning we listened to each other we smiled
and since the day outside was a hundred and seven
were relieved at the coolness of the old marble
"This building must weigh a hundred thousand tons!"
"Yeah, they's a lot of old marble in this place!"
"And it must be ancient, don't you think?"
"Yeah, lookit the old water closet coming down!"
The age of the building could say more than this
about only whites peeing here coughing and spitting
but today our meeting is so easy black and white
we talk and smile and wink like old friends

Arrowhead in the Tar

Since Creeks and Cherokees departed
here long ago, we don't see their life
that filled the fields and parted
the greening hedgerows.
Along the Mohorn Creek the boulders
roll, swept by waters they dipped
to drink and wash their meat.
Silence here is nothing to the call
once echoed through the woods
to the council seat. Leaves and trees
no longer tremble to the dance
and shake of pounding feet.
Today, any set of stones lying
in the grass may produce something
flat, like an arrowhead, but it won't be.
Here on the street I've almost lost
anticipation of finding anything
of what they were when we made
them go. Air stands still, going
towards noon. The city is pouring
tar, asphalt to line the street.
Suddenly I lean toward the hot, acrid
steam and reach for what I've found,
one white sharp edge I pluck
from the burning heap, still warm
in my fingers, and slide it into my palm.

Earth Is a Standing Place

for Andrew Glaze

Earth is a standing place
by what pulls us to it.
Sit all you want, it's
a standing place.
We mull around and go
up mountains at an angle.
We swim out at sea,
flat, kicking. But mostly
we stand on Earth. In our
beds we are horizontal.
We are curious about so
many things, yet we can't
pass up the chance to watch
other standers on the television
or at the baseball game. Football
just takes everybody to
the ground. But do we ever
think of everybody just
standing around? Suppose
there were nothing else
but us just standing. Couldn't
we take a lesson from the force?
Wouldn't we see the odd thing
about it all, the moment when
we finally lift off? And how
curious we haven't, not just yet?

LEAVING THE FARM

for Jim Mersmann

Now they are sold,
the farm is gone,
the catfish are cold
in the bottom of the pond.
You say they were getting
old, anyway, and ate
too many of the other fish.
I wish we had saved
some of their bones to
remember the days we tried
to fool them. But they got
strength from all that food
you threw to them, and
the body behind the head
was bigger than any man's
arm. When hooked, it thrashed
back and forth to pull you in
and cut lines under the dock.
The head, as hard as rock,
could nail another fish
or kill a leaping frog.
We're ignorant of what
catfish can really do.
It woke me up, far from
the farm, to feel this strength
again, so deep and dark
under the pond.

SEEKING MUSIC

for Karim Shamsi-Basha

Out of the desert sands, born of the distant sun,
comes a man, calling in the old way through the lands
a song of sight and sound, pictures of his past
in passing, streets and steeples of a new country
come to, and people, people looking back through
his lens, from India, Iran, Syria, Spain and France
to his new America miles and miles from the desert sands.
Here, too, he comes seeking music in himself, with
hardly a lesson to go by, but determined to understand
his world, the world without violence, the change
that must come over us as searching fingers find their notes
upon the keys. In a new music all sins are forgiven.
The imam sings his Qur'an in all of us, the psalmist
enjoins the mystery of God's melody in a man.
The new music joins us together who are needing
to learn how to sing. So this man, seeking his music,
modifies the world and its senses, from so far back
his calling comes to tell us where he has been,
and who, with his music, we are.

It's Easy for Old Men

It's easy for old men
trembling into words
to sound like pontiffs
making their pronouncements
as if they were simple truths
at last arrived at
how the old masks of childhood
fall off after Halloween
never to be tried on again
or how grandfather's hands they held
in the silence before the service
became the unforgettable sermon

IV

Postcard to Jim Barnes in Missouri

Who invented the postcard anyway
there's hardly room to say
the postcard message slung quickly
to space whatever mind produce
at a certain time in our life
comes the thought I will expire
and something will roll over
and something be left
and music play the songs
we thought of and took for granted
someone will play them over
and sad and love and wind and sun
will dance to indifferent time
all that we were be mixed
in the silence over the house
and along fields where we went
and Grandfather said be quiet now
the rabbit comes see there between rows
it may just be the corn greening
flashed by at the last
or what you said to me
some years ago a packet
in the mail with love

Time

When I saw time sliding by,
in a race I could not win,
the surgeon gave it a quick,
smart crack; whereupon
it rolled over on its back,
and showed me time again.

Samadhi

Now asleep where nothing is,
some have said life is all,
and some have said
Earth is not enough,
we need to be out there;
and some say what's out there
will come its own way;
while others are so busy going
elsewhere, they don't regard
what's here today.

We can't go off to other planets
without thinking what it is
to leave this life. What we achieve
may be all there is, to be out there,
despite efforts to learn what was
nothing before. Yet in a race faster
than they've ever gone, some may
return with what they saw, with looks
of oldest ages lost, upon their faces.

We play music here
as if we were calling out
to space to answer back
or as if we were in space
listening to ourselves being
on Earth, like a piano piece
reaching higher notes,
George Winston maybe,
at the keys, so singular
and spectacular we can
sound, like our one-track
mind about conquering
something while we wait
for someone else to fire
the first shot here on Earth.
Who is out there, so far,
to hear us? We can't send
enough vibrations. It's man
wants to blow himself up.
Possibly his vain desire to be
first was what took us into Iraq
on the imagined assumption
someone had a bomb.
But even if everything there
could explode, the noise would
hardly be heard where stars are.

No One Has Lived Long Enough to Tell

The blank light in the windows
against the wall
says the sun burns this afternoon
and carries away the day
the way it does the ice giant's
blank of frozen North.
You say it will never burn the house
down. Houses are meant to stay.
But rising water taking the shore
will put us farther back
to mountains that no longer
have their ice.
Ice water can drown a house,
and when it recedes, the sun will burn.

PLUMBING TIME

The slow heartbeat of the dripping sink
is now center of the freezing house.
It calculates when the pipes will burst
here in Alabama so long used to mild
winters and warm-air summers.
Nothing can stop a surge of water
against packed-up ice. I've called
the plumbers twice to fix
the bursting pipe. Center of my
kitchen's silent life, the dripping
drops, like the old mantle clock
that couldn't stop in our old house,
and unlike the bursting ice, rolled
my father out of bed to find out
what time it was, if runaway clocks
could tell, and his cold feet
on the floor could stand long
enough to read the clock's hands.
(The old clock went out of sight
by striking thirty-seven times
one night.) Here, I rock
in my winter's time of life
around this dripping in a sink
that has no face, no hands
against our old time's clock,
and doesn't have the power
to chime the hour.

Pine River I

There was once a woman
who loved a river.
The river kept emptying
        itself
near trees and banksides
and floated kayaks and canoes,
never any more a fisherman.
But the river shone and
sparkled as it turned and
hurried under the only
overhangs left. When it
came to a hole, it slowed
to a pool, as if frightened
fish were still there.
Traffic took its toll,
banksides and brush were
chopped away. The woman
went down to the river
every day. Lonely was not
only what a river could be.
She tried to hear what
the river could say, but
that day, all that was lost
was all it could say.

Pine River II

(Michigan)

From the city three men fled to a river.
They did this often enough
they could call themselves fishermen.
Wild as it was, they always knew
they were inside a dream
of the flowing river. When fish were
few, they lived on chanterelles and
wild asparagus. They went to the river
often to hear what it said. There was
music in the riverbed stones and pools
in the bends. Deer came down to listen
with them. Then one day their mantra
changed: "Keep your cigarettes and
matches under your hat." The dam
was gone. Canoes came down, kayaks
whizzed past. Clear water turned brown.
Inside their dream, what did trout see?
Where was it all going, this rush
from their river to the Big Manistee,
and beyond to the big lake like the sea?
They stepped back. Something else was
rushing down. For who would want
to fish without the dream?

I Have Two Clocks

I have two clocks the windup type
the one winds but won't run
the other runs but won't keep time
the first one lies dead in time
frozen in a permanent past
always growing longer
the second makes like a clock
with its tick-tock ticking
this morning I reached for my portable phone
to find the weather and the time
and a voice said, "This is Tuesday
June 18" and shut itself off sharply
as the phone went dead in its little
red dot blinking on and off so there was
no time and no weather only the sun's light
slowly beginning to climb the shutters
opening to a soundless insistence

Iradj and the Didgeridoo

Comes now this music of Australia
you've given me, how the didgeridoo
opens with its thunderous deep voice
and the guitars and violins become one
with the voice of the barking dog
sheepdog and dingo, sometimes the lonely frog
and how the ud has become so far to be
with his brother two thousand years
from each other, singing now heavy and loose
like all the heat waves off one desert
the thunderous voice boils in the sun
and Allah speaks with God
and God and Allah are one
in the jangle-tangle of ruminating music
and every listener has an ear
we have heard this music you and I
and the soul rises up and cannot complain
Rumi himself leans out of his window
catching all we hear

FINDING

Opening the old dresser drawer, finding
the dried red heart-shaped leaf you left,
and the sprig of lavender so carefully wrapped
with a winding weed, and all those dried
Queen Anne's umbels of white florets kept
like fine snow upon a lavender sheet. Then
I took them out to see and hold to the light.
I held the heart fine cracks and slits had
opened up and held it delicately to the sun.
I tried to see what was gone. White florets
still made a circle where they fell. The heart's
shape remained. What would take the years
to tell, is told. Nothing, no, nothing has
changed the love that spoke so well.

HOW TEETH BECOME HISTORY

It's when you're lying there
thinking of each tooth
and the endless brushings,
waiting for the doctor-dentist
to come and poke in, you
focus, somehow, on that one
you always roll your tongue
around, with the sharp edge
from honing with a lower tooth,
the little depression you can't
get any food out of, that
you are suddenly aside from
teeth and regard them as things
in themselves in a strange mouth.
Then their histories begin.
Like an archeologist you calmly
peruse the find: an upper
incisor patched about thirty
years ago, still slicing down;
an upper molar riddled
with silver fillings; lower
front teeth a crooked fencerow
even after successful straightening;
and on either side shining,
the golden molars of wrecked
teeth while dining. To contemplate
the distance between a war and
what is lost requires this distance
to see what remains for use.

IT DARKENED ONE DAY

It darkened one day
the wind blew the sand away
outside the mountain leaves
came down ripping
themselves into a frown
at my door
the sound became a howl
all the valley long
when the roof began to lift
something greater than a rift
between winter's snows
and the mountain's trees
said the world would change
by these pelting blows
perhaps it was she
I had at last turned back
from consuming my self
and the frown hung around
trying to print
its lips on glass

FUNERAL OF AKHMATOVA

(d. March 5, 1966)

From somewhere in a room
of the old cathedral voices sing
angelic Russian women's voices
and softly the candle
great lights in the dome
and the priest comes through the doorway
opening to the people
high icon of Jesus
where he dies and lives
forward the censer
swinging to and fro
and all the soft eyes of Russian
women in tears men turning away
and the girl with dark hair
says Akhmatova's poem
"Go whisper to the waves what's amiss"
and now one kisses the cold Akhmatova
who sleeps a winter of whiteness
where all her poems have risen
and then they begin to lift the coffin
simple wooden box
heavier now than men can bear
up it goes
floating over the people
Yevtushenko turns and lifts
Mayakovsky a memory in the eyes
of faces he lifts her too
voices still singing
and slowly people are in motion
and the box rides over dark figures
of the revolution of war her isolation

and now sadness reaches the woods
black branches against snow
and the slow coffin rises turning
like a leaf on the sea of faces
and down it goes where the priest awaits
hands take shovels begin to dig
one blinks a bright winter sun
and earth holds where earth drops
forever of an afternoon
and the beautiful soul of earth
goes back having heard
last words in the winter snow

TYPING

Six times I tried typing
the manuscript and none perfect
each time a slight mistake
a typo not known something coming
back at me long after
on the seventh *aa* single *o*
turned into an *l* brain not aware
what fingers are doing
shock on the eighth time though
confused me made me get up
walk around the room
to the sessions of sweet
silent thought summoning up
remembrance of things long past
to see if I could figure out
the distance between then and now
and what was making all these mistakes
I heard the voice in my poem
about death how he took away
my wife and mother and father
aunt and uncle so near each other
and was I somewhere else and words
only hitting best they can falling
on the pages as if they would be
understood better even if typed
with the wrong letters
something words could not say
forcing its way on the page
and could I listen to myself
and quietly try to answer back
to what is wrong in the way
things come out

THE PENDULUM MOVES OFF

(A Prophecy)

As our Earth turns in space
at seventeen miles per second,
it makes the rounds of its own life,
even as it did before us.
It needs the sun for seeds to sprout,
its oil to make coal, its weather to water
trees and plants, rivers where water can go.

Over Earth today, we think we can't go back
to where we were while we were stripping
the land and pervading air with carbon rain.
We could not have foreseen then, what is
here now, time running out for beleaguered
man, the logjam where greed and hesitation
reign and we are following. It's a question
how long it will take us to change our mind
as the weather changes. What we've taken out
doesn't come back. Millions of years seem
nothing to our frontal attack. It's a race
between fires that occur and fires we make,
warming waters we don't want and air crackling
with smoke and burning embers.

So the garden goes down as if Adam
has had his look in, but never gone back.
No gardenias in May, only a few struggle
to appear in September, the holly bush loses
its leaves to sticks, Asian pear goes down.
Trees from the South are moving northwest,
birds in Pennsylvania mysteriously disappear.
We might as well ask where have honeybees

gone. *The cause of climate change must be*
our cause to change everywhere. The long
dark foreboding cloud of smoke from
the West penetrates air toward you and me,
while rainforests in Brazil burn haphazardly
and people on Arctic tour ships watch wistfully
as once landlocked ice slides into the sea.

The backup speed of the dragonfly is so
rapid we barely perceive as it goes, whereas
that of humans into their past is so slow, we
hesitate to know. What we have taken away
takes us away. We all play the low mode
bassoon of loss. Now a great pendulum moves
off, with us on it in our agony of uncertainty,
as if it has won, turning by itself to swing
in its long irreversible arc around the sun.

V

Unwinding the Clock

Il est trois heures ici,
and it can't be more *trois heures*
than it is. The second hand holds
back slightly as it rounds the clock
losing itself enough to be holding
time back and never winning more
than it takes to return an afternoon
or morning or some time late at night
in the dark when no one is looking.
I've watched this clock for years
and years and never seemed to see
a difference or worry about when
or if, and yet I know something is
turning, something in the very word
I say, that says there is a motion
but not a time, whose essence I could
get to, if I knew what made mountains
or skyscrapers or put the waves in motion.
The human effort might win out at last,
were it not for the wars and floods
and winds that put us humans on the rack.
The single click of the rifle trigger is
like the second hand of the clock
but won't really tell us time and buries
a secret that harries our day and worries
our night. Human greed may hurry another
to press the button to illumine the sky,
and seconds will seem like years and then
centuries and no time at all. And the essence
of what was time will be gone.

STILL THERE

Here is the grassland, and the road
through it, so bristly-bright green
and the curve of the road so natural
its gray one-lane seems as if it's
always been there. It's a road to
somewhere, and the blue purple-pink
horizon far away. I like the way grass
can sway. You want to be in it. It calls
for you to smother face in green, a tree
beside the road, grass as far as you can
see. How smooth its shadow-carpet goes,
its small, fuzzy dandelion remnant before,
before wind, before morning, and you
don't resist feeling you are not alone.

VAN GOGH'S POEM

It could have been a bud of green he saw
one troubling day beside an ash heap.
In the only painting of "The Sower"
with a tree in it, Van Gogh darkens
the human as dark as the large tree
trunk that dominates the scene, in
a field just becoming green. A spot
of brighter green appears beside
the sower as if a light has gone on
in the dark of body and tree. Where
limbs have been cut off, the trunk
has sprouted strong shoots that
pierce the air. It's fair to ask what
Van Gogh is planting in this scene.
A poem how earth in the spring,
the human, the dominating trunk
and the round evening sun are
the hope of things that get planted
and have already begun. We are
waiting for things to emerge, and
the poem is the emergence of spring,
just as perception and thought converge
in a metaphor in the making, and
we, the observer, are urged to feel
the change. For Van Gogh, nothing
could better depict the hope of man
and earth. In this poem the sower is
not merely planting seeds, as in the
other sower poems, but with powerful
colors and some clever restraints,
Van Gogh creates his poem in paint.

TWO TREES

In Birmingham, on the old Savoy Road
you can get to it coming up a hill
or rounding a curve from the other way.
The oak is old, of course, so big
around the middle and nearly taking
up the road, as you would suppose.
And of course, some limbs cut off,
sticking out like arms missing
at the elbows. You can see some
scars from drivers missing the road
as they stared at the old giant's limbs
looming overhead and missed the only
opening beneath a spreading canopy.
On off-days, though, children feeling
its grandeur join hands around its
still-growing body.
Tree two is a marvel in Homewood
of twisted and knotted trunk, a red maple,
and rare to see such a tree as this.
It bends at precarious angle to share
its leaves with passing pedestrians
at a corner. How it sticks out and
someone says, "The crooked tree,
it's greening again!" Its trunk is so
ugly, all knobs and see-throughs, wicked
as witchery in winter, calm as a bent
candlestick, leaning to greet you.
Of all the trees we could say are ugly,
this one will scare you quickly. But
then, passing it summer and winter,
it speaks another language, how things
of nature can remind us that we stare,
and then happily realize how something

so ugly can become a friend. We look
for it as we approach the corner. We see
it in the rearview as we move down
the street. Somehow, later, we think
of it among all the things we've forgotten
before the day has ended. It's good we
think something will always be there.
As with the old oak, I've seen people
stop to touch it, running their hands
over it, as if it were something alive
and needed people to go on living.

LEAVES ARE TURNING

The leaves are turning
how they fade now
between the window frames
commanding all the sights
pink at first then yellow
an adagio to August suns
then orange and finally red
and dun-color brown
come winter when only
a few are left to sing
for now they look back
satisfied with summer
each leaf lifting gently
for the fall we know will come
staccato-like with the rain,
allegretto in the sun

Father to Daughter

We listen for each other now
sure our voices remember her
who is gone who still lives
in this house by silence kept
and the blue curtains her color
for everything she believed in
and the shamrock that blooms
profusely now at the kitchen window
that had only dark leaves before
I count those sounds in the night
tap or shuffle of a bathrobe
as if she were still traipsing
the front room or a hallway getting used
to the darkness she would finally know
so we call each other you and I
and we talk eagerly here over lunch
looking for her in our eyes and faces
when we meet and speak but don't say
as if to answer for the full life
that she did not have with us
that we would have had with her

POEM IN THE PIANO

for Sasha Kasman

It is all a living
for the moment to play.
The poem is already a memory
in the mind of the player.
The poem starts with *images*
of Debussy, soon taken up
with a Bach *partita*, followed
by raucous Medtner and Stravinsky,
the *Rhapsody on a Theme of
Paganini*, to the quiet place
in Prokofiev's *Romeo and Juliet*,
all one poem in the graceful note
of time in the sublimity and wars
of self we listen to, as we listen for.
There is always some of the music
playing itself backward toward
the composer's exploratory fingers.
In your fingers is the lost self
that returns to us when you play,
and we are found again. And
some music is left over,
the notes of the pianist as she
turns to us, still hearing
the notes she has played.
And the ones next day, as she
walks along, singing her own
song, that does not end.

COMING BACK

Where I made my turn that day
it was long rows of bare trees
in an old pecan orchard and a rail
fence. As I drove, a fox appeared
beside the road. His sudden leaping
made me slow to a speed we could go.
His magnificent tail flowed through
openings in the rails. I steered eerily
as tiny black feet and tail effortlessly
floated along. I know I saw *him*, but
what did he see in the side of my car
as far as he could see? Or was he like
a dog, running to bark at my wheel?
Fox and man are nothing new. The
game was on—seen in this race they
could make a pair and maybe place.
In trying me, he increased the pace.
Whenever I got close, the car might
take a blow from the fence. Whether
he enjoyed this I'll never know. At
times I was loping with the fox in the
slow-motion flow of bodies, as they go.
He seemed to have no sense of ego or
pride in showing off. We kept this
flittering up for about a mile, till I,
turning left, thought I saw him smile
as he calmly veered right, and his tail
went out of sight. He left me in a cold
sweat. This was no question of who was
fooling who, or how he went, or how
my eye was bent to see him to the end.
We know who won. It was black, red-
brown and white all the way. Today what

fox might feel was all his own and far off;
for me the wonder of being this close to
a moving fox, was in keeping to the wheel.
Could I have done this without a car?
I don't know how to run. I remember him
like a dream. From where he came, I was
certain he spoke for something I'd forgotten.

INTO THE STREAM

for Ted Colson

Fishing is not all there is to the river.
It comes to coming down to it,
The secret roads one takes all week in
the mind that anticipate the first
plunge in, and even above
the hips, the clear, clean water as if
going back to birth again, sweet
fern in the air so rare a smell, and
all the leaves and trees of the bends
where lines can go deeply in.
Catching one was only half what
you might see when he didn't see
you. It was the miracle of Earth
itself that could produce a fish
we could believe in. All the stories
of fish came back to us then, even
the one so bold that made us
strive to be fishers of men.

RACCOON

I was on the path from deep water
when he looked up at me with
a child's face in an old man's. He
stood in the way, over three feet
tall, eyes immediately connected
to mine, and didn't move an inch.
I couldn't pass him in the long grass.
His look was so knowing, he knew
I had something in the creel. What
was it in him prompted me to open
it I still ponder, even to the potential
ferociousness of his shining teeth.
But it wasn't that—perhaps he knew
me better than I knew him, an old
raccoon practicing his skill on
an innocent man. I reached in and took
out a still fresh rainbow and made
an offering to him, which he received
in his paws like two hands, and
whiskers and all, he bumbled down
to the river to wash and eat the fish.
Above the hum of the river I could
hear his earnest splashing. Giving
him the fish was a giving back to
the river, and I was as much a part
of the river as he was.

AMANITAS

Down to the river through the pathway
of pines in the fluttering sunlight
I come to the place where I can cross,
but on the Pine River now I pass a
large clump of mysteriously white
mushrooms, *Amanita verna* (in the
South *Amanita virosa*) known as
the destroying angel, one of the most
poisonous mushrooms in the world.
Pass them reverently, I say, and I do,
and over rushing waters safely.

Much later, farther down, and fishing
too late, I turn into the warming dark
but have no light and struggle to
find the way, knowing now I'm lost.
There's something final in the way
the heated air smells different in the
closing night. Moving along the bank,
one misstep, and you could go in
overhead. Inching now along in
a growing sweat and hoping I don't
misstep, I see what seems a pale
glow coming from the river. Closer
I go, deep water or no; glow becomes
a light, and I hear water skittering
over stones. I'm back at the shallows
and the Amanitas now so full I can
read stones in the riverbed. Rising
from the river, I pass again the silent
glowing Amanitas.

LOVE LETTER

The bird's beak that I resent
in the tomatoes
has carved and left me
a perfect heart in a tomato.
I know the bird it was.
He sings at night
all the tunes he's heard
all day and won't stop.
But why this bird has chosen
a tomato to make another
mark and one that only I
would know can only come
from his intent to mock.
Yet how would he have
known my love for a tomato
or any love I chose
was exactly what he carved?
I haven't seen him for a week.
He's usually so neat and quick
to spy a meal and find the one
he would like to steal.
His absence makes me wonder
still further if this heart wasn't
his last reminder of his artistry
in tomato and that I could miss
him, too. This doesn't end.
You can't ever aim at a bird,
their flights and skirmishes
being so much their own.

That picture now, of the old house
on the curving rutted road in winter,
shows the devoted nun in black covering
the distance to the swing set and laundry
hanging out in the wind, snow on the roof,
the big maple full of it springing skyward,
and all the trees beside in snow-mist
like a fairytale inviting the stranger
to its dark windows and hopeless look.
She brings her leather case of medicine
and Word and will not stumble in crossing
over a drainage ditch. Barbed wire hidden
in a fencerow cannot stop her. She knows
someone in the house awaits her. The scene,
like a Rembrandt etching, makes its lines
and holds the winter. We don't see the will
of the heart that opens towards the house,
nor how many winters she has weathered
to make this visit. Her heart has its meaning
and blessed message, for she will bring light
to the windows, child to the yard, and family
to love, as spring comes to winter, and home
　　　　to the dove.

LITTLE DRIED FLOWER

From out of the pages of *Walden*
it comes, its long skinny stem
stiff and dried, its flower folded
over like a head looking down,
its tiny interwoven petals closed
and still clinging to their stem.
It was when I read the words
"I cannot come nearer to God
and Heaven/ Than I live to
Walden even" that in my prayer
in the afternoon at the Pond
God presented me a single flower
without leaves, and I could say
it, too, in the closing hour.

LEAVES

for Isadore Seltzer

The leaves rise up
in their own tornado
and like the driven snow
across the yard they go
hurrying to their landing place
in hedgerow and cherry laurel
birds huddle in what they know
heave and heave the wind begins
the way we watch the year's end
there's no momentary stay
against the howling up the driveway
that throws yellow and red and brown
a million times into the dark wood
behind the house and on the ground
these may lie still upon a roof
but in a moment lift again
for the drive that turns the world
and nails earth to Earth again and again

ACKNOWLEDGMENTS

Grateful thanks to the editors of the following publications, where some of these poems first appeared, sometimes in altered form:

5AM: "No One has Lived Long Enough to Tell"
The Chariton Review: "What the Lake Said"
Kinship: "Kinship 2012"
Poetry South: "Arrowhead in the Tar," "Arvo Pärt Plays from the Radio," "Coming Back," "Finding," "Frog," "Grandpa Wears Neckties," "Houses We've Built," "How Teeth Become History," "I Saw Time," "I Was Up in My Room," "Leaving the Farm," "Lines for Maurice McNamee, SJ," "Listening," "On a Child's Waking at Night," "Putting in the Flag," "Raspberries and Milk," "Seeking Music," "Walden: A Glimpse"
POMPA: "Father to Daughter," "I Have Two Clocks," "Leaves," "Leaves Are Turning," "Messiaen's Quartet for the End of Time," "Taking the Trees," "Typing"
Valley Voices: "The Boy Fishing," "Broken Heart," "Brothers," "Earth Is a Standing Place," "Funeral of Akhmatova," "Homeless," "It Darkened One Day," "My Return," "The Pendulum Moves Off," "Pine River I," "Pine River II," "Plumbing Time," "Still There," "A Tall Tale," "Two Trees," "Vicksburg on the Mississippi," "Where Poetry Goes"

Gracious thanks to Jianqing Zheng, Jim Mersmann, and Randy Blythe; Kimberly Davis and Linda Parsons for their generous and perceptive editing of these pages; and Radcliffe Squires in memoriam.

About the Author

Theodore Haddin is a poet, editor, and emeritus professor from the University of Alabama at Birmingham. His poems have appeared in a chapbook, *The River and the Road*, and a book, *By a Doorway, in the Garden*. His poems have appeared in *5AM*, *The Birmingham Poetry Review*, *The Chariton Review*, *Valley Voices*, *POMPA*, *Poetry South*, and in three anthologies, *Alabama Poets*, *Contemporary Literature in Birmingham*, and *Whatever Remembers Us*. His reviews on American literature and poetry have been in *Valley Voices*, *The Anniston Star*, *Birmingham Poetry Review*, *Southern Humanities Review*, *South Atlantic Review*, and *Western American Literature*. A professionally trained violinist, Haddin has performed locally and supported several music organizations, including The Arianna String Quartet and individuals in Berlin and St. Louis. At UAB, The Humanities Forum he founded and directed has been named in his honor as The Theodore Haddin Forum for the Arts and Sciences.

www.ingramcontent.com/pod-product-compliance
Lightning Source LLC
Chambersburg PA
CBHW022013080426
42733CB00007B/584